Walking through the Forest

love, loss & other tall trees

wildflower edition

Elizabeth Ann

isbn provided by Library and Archives of Canada
isbn: 978-1-988750-02-6

Cover created by Islam Farid (islamfarid.net)

this edition is dedicated to
those of you walking through your
own forest

may you find wisdom in storms
solace in sunsets
rest in meadows
& beauty throughout your entire journey

Crystal,

thank you for supporting
my writers journey.
I hope you find healing
in these words.

:) liz

I see the trees
9

the forest is dark
23

making peace with the mud
43

with healing comes the sun
63

planting seeds
77

watering flowers
91

a meadow called love
105

author's note

When I released the original edition of Walking, I was sitting in serious pain. In fact, I bailed on selling at markets afterwards because I had recently had the "let's get divorced" talk and needed a few moments for the inward honoring of the sacredness of my ending marriage.

Like all things, as I walked further away from the experience I could see with more clarity. I realize now that I pushed the release of the original Walking hastily because I was using the excitement of self-publishing a book to get through an otherwise painful situation. Publishing was a light in the darkness.

In this, the wildflower edition, I have re-vamped my journey. Some poems from the original edition made it while some did not. I have also re-organized the flow– like I said before, I was hasty in my original organization and some poems were fillers. I value the opportunity to correct that. This time around I've been firm with myself– no fillers. I have created art I am incredibly proud of.

In addition, I have added a chapter to the end. I was very much in the forest when I released the original and had no idea of what was to come.

And what came after the forest was beautiful and difficult and moonlit and I wanted a place to celebrate that.

So much of my journey has been about
realizing I am loved in a manner I accept; I
have power in my relationships and in my
life. The newly added last chapter speaks to
some of my learning. The last chapter also
describes my introduction to a bliss I have
not previously experienced.

To those of you who have supported my writing
journey either in part or entirety

thank you.

Thank you for allowing me to be flawed.
Thank you for giving me a space to improve
myself.
Thank you for encouraging me & supporting
me.

I love you.

Xo,

elizabeth

I see the trees...

they say
actions speak
louder than words
but I don't know
if I believe them
because his
lackofaction and
wordslikeknives
piercing my
fragile skin
left quite the
impact

I have lost the desire

to be stabbed repeatedly

by his words

please God

soothe my wounded spirit

watching warm air
v a p o r i z e
in front of a cold window
reminds me
what it's like to love him

he thrives on
making me feel
as little and insignificant
as he feels
about himself
    (and I'm over it)

the casualty
with which he tosses me
' to the

                                  side

makes him dangerous
to me and my heart

pricked by another thorn

his love is as cold
as the ice cubes in my freezer

yet his words carry the
burn of a million suns

our disintegration
            was not for a lack of love

      but that doesn't make me want to stay here
in this weird
            uncomfortable place
                        of not knowing

just makes me scratch harder
                  at the walls
                        to get out

seared in my heart
is the fear
he will remain on the
Land of Withholding Love

I wanna blow that land to pieces
watch the fiery ash float into the sunset
and declare myself the destroyer

touch me. please just touch me

he said he loved me

but he didn't

how could he

when he didn't love himself

turns out these plants are poisonous

our bodies pressed together
breathing the same air
his tongue dancing with mine

I loved when he wrapped his strong hands
around the base of my neck while
he kissed me
his fingers weaved in my hair
felt like he was trying
like he wanted to be there

the last time we kissed
we knew we were breaking
almost broken
but pretended we weren't

did I do that for him?
did he do that for me?

or did we do that for ourselves

one last dance before the fall

months into our separation he told me
he had a problem with throwing away items
he still needed

material possessions:
shoes
furniture
electronics
clothes

                                        me

months previous he'd stood with me
the most handsome I'd ever seen him
and as he looked me in the eyes
in front of our loved ones he promised to
walk through all things with me

I hadn't realized then that to him
walking through all things
was the equivalent of
throwing me out with the trash
once I no longer served a purpose
that was comfortable for him

I know this now

             remaining comfortable

        is the song of the coward

the sadness drilled a hole into my heart
as deep as it is wide
and the pain filled it with fire

burn baby, burn

the forest is dark...

we came together
two broken souls
desperate for love &
unintentionally we weaved
an overcomplicated tapestry
requiring several seam rippers
and thread snippers
to make sense of the mess

with every snip
of every thread
I felt the stab and pull
in the center of me
like the snippers were
cutting my skin open and
pulling him out of my soul

I don't think this will end beautifully
our kinks smoothed out
on a carefully painted canvas
full of color and love

I think this will end with
our bodies ripped to pieces
floating down a dirty street
in rivers of our warm blood

in the shadows I see monsters

I crumple onto my bed

                          defeated

I throw my arms above my head
focus on my beating heart &
imagine blood pouring from my wrists

I want the pain to stop
I want a way out of this

                          an escape

I am tired of always coming back to this place

     this place I must claw myself out of

                     quicksand

I'm in the dirty resistance
caked on mud leftover lava &
last nights glitter
silence & a winding road
silence & nothing but my thoughts
silence & reminders of how you want me to be
everything in threes
you. with your discontent and demons
destroying everything you touch
including me

day old booze too many cigarette burns
dried up memories
broken promises spiteful touches
tornados of betrayal
a body used split open bled dry
flashbacks of bar parking lots
the fights & the sex
drugged up hazes cold laced cruelty
dragged down to hell
loss my old friend
the only reliable relationship
period of mourning clawing my way back
resilience
silence
no one's yelling
no one's stabbing
no one's killing
no one's here

the dirty resistance
tastes like resolve is building in the
back of my throat
stand up brace myself look around

no one's here

... the ellipsis after his apology is
underwhelming ...

... does he think the dot dot dot fills the void
that arrived when he left?
like all those dots makes the apology
more grandiose *dot*
          more genuine *dot*
                   more forgivable *dot*
              ...

I'm still aching in silence
I'm still wondering where he went
I'm still crying myself to sleep wishing I
could reach out to him

no number of dots holds me like he can...

I lay in bed
a pile of skin, bones &
broken hope
begging God for strength to
walk through this pain

I don't know how to exist in these shadows

a stack of mail sits on my stairs
something addressed to him on top of the pile

I wish he'd change his address

receiving his mail reminds me
he once lived here
and how empty my bed is
now that he's gone

I filled his side with pillows

I want to call him
pick a fight with him
yell at him
tell him how much he hurt me
hang up on him
drive to his house
& kiss his stupid face

these shadows are making me crazy

I feel like I'm missing a limb
like I have an open wound and
sometimes the wound is scabbed over
and sometimes without warning
the scab is torn off
and I'm just there

                                  alone
blood pouring from my wound

as I lay in a puddle of my blood
all I can think about
is how unfinished life seems without him

like a stem without a bloom
or a tree without a branch
or a cloud without a rainstorm

and oh how painfully I miss him

I'm waiting for something I might not get

an apology
an explanation
a declaration of love
a promise to honor vows

companionship
intimacy
connection

I'm waiting for light
for truth
for openness

I'm waiting for something I might not get

setting myself on fire to see in the dark

I stretch with my whole body
and hope I will pop and release

the sadness
the longing
the fear
the betrayal
the loneliness
the hurt

I'm still waiting to pop

I've read about some people knowing the moment their significant other turns to another direction but for me our dance felt more like I never fully had him, like he always had one foot out the door ready to run. a sprinter prepared for his mighty dash. I wonder how standing in a room with him would feel each end of a string tied to our naked ring fingers. I wonder if we'd be uncomfortable seeing the connection to each other. a powerful visual of the vows we took yet can't seem to honor. I wonder if he'd slice my finger off to get away from me and I wonder if I'd be glad he left, relieved to have solitude for my pain. I wonder if he'd miss me the way I miss him, wanting to reach out but scared of rejection

can I have my finger back?

I want to burn

the strings attaching

him to my heart

and lay in my blood

until my heart has

scarred over

and I am free of him

you
with your foot out the door

me
with this hole in my heart

you
turning away to avoid watching me bleed out

me
gasping for breath as I hit the ground

if you never meant to stay
how dare you knock down my walls
burrow through my arteries
electrify my nerves
make a room for yourself
make me think you were safe
make me think I could make a home out of you

you
with your foot out the door

six months later
my ring finger feels naked
                              exposed & lonely

I still catch myself wondering what feels off
and when I realize my hand is twitching
for a moment I mourn for the loss of us

when I hang with my married friends
glitzy adorned fingers flashing while they
tell stories

                  I feel like an intruder

the first time we all went out for girls night
after he left I was embarrassed so I hid my
hand under the table because my naked ring
finger felt like a flashing neon sign around
my neck:

                  FAILED MARRIAGE

                  FAILED MARRIAGE

                  FAILED MARRIAGE

the moon is gorgeous
lighting the sky like a
beacon calling for my freedom
but all I can concentrate on
is the monsters clawing through
my insides making a mess of my organs
sharp claws and jagged teeth
tearing through my heart my mind
drowning in blood and pain

the moon is gorgeous
its glow lighting the place I fall
defeated amongst wildflowers and blades
tree pollen and poison
my skin delicate sinew
tough enough to heal but soft enough to scar
and scared enough to never forget
how I got here

these monsters have made me prisoner
to my own mind and body
to have freedom so close I can taste
the sugary sweetness of flying away
rocks thrown out of my shoes
air swirling between my toes
my only map the clouds and the wind
doesn't seem fair when I'm constantly
pulled back by these damn heathens
who squeeze blood one pore at a time
who make damn sure I'm paying attention
to them
who ruthlessly torture in slow motion
until finally falling into blades
seems like relief
the wildflowers I normally find refuge in
mocking me

the moon is gorgeous
but all I see and feel tonight is darkness
weighing me down when I stop moving
slicing my body
       my mind
       my heart with dread

with its crooked claw
with its inability to love
with its uneasiness to trust
with its memories of trauma
with its chains and loneliness

claw through my rotting wounds
pull the throbbing clotted blood from me
watch as the red stain runs down your wrists
a product of a flawed society
a product of men treating women as objects
a product of the war on a woman and
the rights to her body
the right to sexual pleasure
the right to consent
a perpetual state of self-validation
did that happen
was that real
was he intentional or did I misunderstand
did he use my vulnerability for his gain
I thought he was my friend
am I worthless am I confused
their consistent violation by manipulation
the creation of the whisper telling me not to
trust him. telling me to self-sabotage.
telling me to remain uninhabitable.
telling me to run
I have grown tired of the whisper. of the
perpetual need for self-validation
was I right to feel dirty
was I right to feel used
was I right to express myself
was I right to seek healing
was I right

making peace with

the mud...

they call me in a rage. assuming they know the
answer without asking the question.
or they hide. afraid of ink on paper.

insecurity runs rampant, their confidence a
façade marching from their bellies up their
throat rolling off their tongue. fake. they
might fool others but they do not fool me.

so again I will say this poem is not about you

this poem is about me. my story. my breath. my
heart. this poem is both fierce and delicate. a
mirror image of myself. an account of how I
forced myself off the floor and took my life
back.

this poem is me standing in front of you
looking you straight in the face with wide
open icy blue eyes while I tell you I am no
longer a pawn in your game.
I am a whole human available for whole love
and not an ounce of anything less.
this poem is my victory flag.
its pole a clever combination of cool steel
and burnt wood. a reminder of where I have
come from and what I am made of.
this poem is a reminder that I will respond to
the wind as a victory flag does.

mercilessly, with intention.

I handle her with care
aware of the places to not touch her
respecting the love I have for her

unlike the shame he drowned me in
touching me where I am most feminine
he was a coward
sneaking his touches in
pretending he was innocent

He Is Guilty.
and i was insignificant

an object
unworthy of respect
unworthy of safety
of honesty. of love
unworthy

small
uncared for

I will not do that to her

to the men that have hurt me

all I see after experiencing
you is the shell of a man in
denial of the damaged little boy
he really is

I'm sorry you're in so much pain

you cannot justify your cruelty by
telling me you treat me this way
because you love me

"tough love" is what I think you called it
"I'm doing this because I love you"
"so you don't get hurt in the future"

right   let's make something clear

kicking someone when they're down isn't love

it's abuse

you treat me this way not because you love me
but because you fear how high I will fly once I
get up off the floor

wings as wide as the horizon

a tree
abundant with leaves
appears to be a safe place
to rest my weary heart & release my sadness

the sun
hearing my woes
stretches her warmth to provide me
with comfort

the tree mocks my pain

listens to me cry before
pretending she has an axe in her side
so the sunlight will shine
on her instead

rooted in narcissism

I am a product of
alcoholism
narcissism
shame
fear

codependency and insecurity
flow through my veins

I crave boundaries while fearing them

no wonder healthy relationships
are so damn unattainable

they beat me with branches
& got mad at me for bruising

realizing I'm selling myself out again
in hopes I will be acknowledged
brings a heaviness so dark
I stop seeing starlight

I don't like this part of the forest

I crave the stars

they have all either
abused me or replaced me &
most have done both

his loud angry walk out our door
was the end of a lot of things
among them
the assignment of my worth
from someone else

I sat in the boldly quiet devastation
absorbing all the pain
and felt the grief tear open
all my wounds

it was then in silent screams
I promised myself
my price tag would
never again
be written by a man

climbing trees one by one

I am terrified
of these butterflies
flittering around
in their self-obsession

boasting beautifully colored wings
shimmering in the sunlight

covered in poison
toxic enough to kill me

they called me Beth
until 12 years of age
when after careful consideration of whom I
wanted to become at this intersection between
child and young woman I bravely declared at
church one rainy morning:

"I would like to be called Liz now"

rain pounded the windshield on the drive
home after my vulnerable Sunday declaration.
I watched the wipers struggle while he turned
to me and said:

"girls called Liz are Bitches"

and so began my ascent into womanhood

I painted my young face with war paint
pierced the ground with battle flags &
left pieces of my young naive self behind
as I fought my way up the mountain

I would gladly be a bitch if it meant

men like him stayed away from me

he surrounded himself with
bright red warning flags
yet I was so desperate for love
I chose not to acknowledge them

does that make this my fault?

the scared little girl I was raised to be
will always live inside me

no amount of
                    therapy
                    self-love
                    spirituality
                    acceptance
will abolish her

she is a part of me
                    and I her

I will always fear
                    doing something wrong
                    anger
                    not being good enough
                    hostility

I will not wash my body in the
blood of my enemy
I will not allow myself
to be invaded by
his inability
to finish a thought
to nurture a feeling

I will not be threatened by
his armor of anger

I will not find nourishment
in the despair he encompasses

in the depths of hell
he recruits his army from

I could sense he didn't want to ask
but I said yes anyways

and the pit that was born that evening
into my heart
stayed
until a few short months after our wedding
when he left me

I wasn't surprised he left

I just didn't think he'd go that soon

profound sadness follows the realization

that I might never again get a sentiment of
love from him. I think of those scenes in
movies where a human's genetic makeup
changes and the camera zooms into the body
for us to watch the change occur. strands of
genetic code are put through intense
modification, shifting from what they once
were to what they now are. anytime I've
watched this happen I've thought about how
painful a revolution of that magnitude must
be. a change in genetic make-up has got to
hurt.

this morning I laid in bed, in that place
between awake and sleep, and talked myself
through waking up in this new reality;
waking up in a world where sentiments of love
from him are no longer an option and I could
feel the strands of DNA snap and twist and
transform and I was right.

hurts like hell

between dark places & searching for my worth
                                    I lost count

one after another endless stream
desperation
searching for worth
giving pieces of myself away to
everyone not interested in keeping

the burning out of light
that last lick of flame before the
disintegration
another drink
another hit
another one-night stand

searching for worth this way will never work

worth will never be found in
                        the pockets of broken

the first real love song I sang to myself

pungent air violated my senses as I walked
into his garden. the blood he waters his
flowers with seeped beneath the cracked
concrete. beauty was desolate just like his
love.

the crawling vines seemed desperate for an
escape route. their stains turning the once
bright greenery to rust.

I identify with their despondence
I want out as well

flashbacks to friday morning's misery have
sunk their talons into me. blood on the
bathroom floor. the walls. ceiling.
him. soaking in a claw footed tub. all rose
thorns and poison ivy. I never understood why
he did that. surely, the toxins scorched his
skin.

overwhelming melancholy flows through my
veins. how can I walk away knowing how much I
love him. how do I grow flowers from this.

pleading with God

self-loathing. a dark room. a disheartened
shadow. begging God please can I feel loved?
please can I feel safe? consistent like the
beat of my heart and the rise and fall of my
lungs

the unbecoming

the next day the air shifted around him. I
didn't know what it meant until hours later
when it all came crashing down

inwards

numbness dragged through my body leaving a
searing pain in its wake.
I retreat inwards.
I spend days silently screaming. nights
writhing in pain.
the burn radiated slowly through my being
leaving a life I no longer recognized.
While sifting through the remains I see so
many pieces no longer fit.

I reassemble my life. myself.

I realize while doing dishes one evening the
unbecoming was a gift from God. a loud
message that my safety is important. that I am
loved. I sob while scrubbing the pots.

with healing comes

the sun...

as the sun nestled into the clouds
at the end of a long day I thought about
endings
about my endings
about him and his cruelty
how the moon would stretch herself
to light the way for my escape

I never thanked her

by the time I left covered in wounds
I was too ragged to feel anything but pain
so over and over
the moon shone bright for me
thanklessly
hoping I would find freedom

I've come a long way since my only stability
was pain and light of the moon

every night while she shone beautifully
above me I cried myself to sleep

a prisoner in myself

when I finally became free
she shone red with love for me
revived. grateful. proud of a job well done.

she saved me
and I never thanked her

thank you sweet moon

burn with the ashes

float away with the wind

land on the petals of

wildflowers

become one with the meadow

my plan, now that he's gone

my therapist demanded I give him the pillow
so I'd stop hiding behind it

I begrudgingly complied
(I think I growled and
threw it at him)

sitting on that couch
I felt naked
exposed
unprotected

it was in that moment I knew I found
the place I needed to be

thank you for taking the pillow

may the pain burn &
my breath escape me
may tears containing sadness
from my spirit pour from my eyes
allow me to sit in silent screams while I
feel my Heart On Fire

as I sit still in this burning I
feel my heart shrivel
a vessel of ash and paper
& when I have learned what I need to
from this pain let me feel my ashy heart
d i s i n t e g r a t e
into the space between my ribs

as I wipe the sadness from my face &
embrace this lesson for healing
may my lungs fill with air newly oxygenated
by the trees I turn to for wisdom

may I have gratitude for
this pain
this lesson
this release of sadness from my spirit

Amen

I am no longer a vessel
to be used only for
a man's satisfaction
& then thrown to the side

easily abused
easily ignored
easily neglected

this wildflower has bloomed

my heart has been wounded but
I lay in bed at night half asleep
overwhelmed with love

I know I am healing

I place my hand on my heart & fall asleep
with a thankful smile on my face

I am learning love is so much bigger than a
man who backed out on his promise to me.
bigger than pain or sadness or wounds from
abuse. love is bigger than I could have ever
dreamed to imagine

I will soldier on with my healing heart
I will bravely immerse myself in love

I will learn to forgive

this poem is a token of love I will place on a
chain & wear close to my heart. I will hold it
when the forest gets dark & I crave faith to
get me through

this will all end in my favor

take stock of the damage
breathe
with hand on heart
feel it beat and pulse
there may be damage
but my heart is beating

beating heart means healing heart

honor painful moments
cry when necessary
be brave
be kind to self
be kind to others
cling to faith
remember to pray
step by step
walk yourself through

you got this, girl

instructions given in self-love

grief:

the process of change &

acceptance that occurs within

someone's spirit

following the loss of love

and oh, how it changed me

tears streaming
heart pounding
eyes closed

focus on my breath
slow down
breathe deep
breathe slow
breathe steady
focus on my body
focus on my heart
focus on my energy
focus on my spirit
focus

breathe deep
I am at peace with
the past, present &
future
breathe slow
I forgive you
breathe steady
I will be brave in
love
focus on my body
be brave

I am open
breathe deep
I welcome love into
my life
breathe slow
I welcome love into
my heart
breathe steady
my inner child is
safe with me
focus on my body
I am safe with me
focus on my energy
I have faith in
God's plan for me
focus on my spirit
I am open
slow down
I forgive you
breathe deep
I forgive me
breathe slow

open eyes
breathe deep
breathe steady

I found reprieve among
the background of a quiet meadow

I planted my feet
felt them take root
with the wildflowers around me

filled my lungs with freshly cleaned air
thanked God for this meadow &
waited in contemplative silence
while the rains poured
and my soul healed

how I became the tallest tree

self-love
prayer
pain
loneliness
bravery
solidarity
authenticity
acceptance
growth
intuition
spirituality
friendship
introspection
meditation
therapy
wisdom
love
forgiveness
compassion
respect
faith

wildflowers

planting seeds...

I long to be one with the earth

I long to curl my toes into the dirt
feel the rain hydrate my skin &
watch wildflowers grow from my scars

grounded

I want to place all the pain
associated with him
into a box in the corner
firmly close the lid
and live life without it

forgiveness

I looked at my heart and I said

heart
I know you're tired

but now is not the time to demand
your best walls
stand up straight
stand up tall
stand up strong
stand up ready to protect you

now is the time
to absorb love
to rest in peace
to breathe with bravery
to wake up your wildness
to let your softness run over

if I could rewrite
my vows to him
I would promise to
love him when he was
unlovable

seed

the silence that follows
the disintegration
of ashy flame licked hearts
is a sacred place of learning

sprout

all that will be left
when the flames cease
and the ashes fall
will be space
& wisdom for
wildflowers

and oh, how wild they'll grow

bloom

If I could rewrite
my vows to him
I wouldn't

I would soak up the sun
that warm September day
with faith that God had me

that the journey in front of me
would be worth it

that I would be engulfed in flames
they would dance down my throat
burn the innermost sacred parts
of myself that I kept hidden from the world

that my baptism of fire would
burn my pain away
and leave me with an oasis
for the wildest of flowers

the price of his damage to me
has been my slogan
on my walk through this forest

I have climbed trees
waded through swamp water
& fell into fire pit embers
all while singing my
song of healing

but without warning
the air around me changed

because with the force
of a lightning bolt striking the tallest tree
I understood

I have hurt him as much as he has hurt me

I am so sorry

I'm just feeling so no thank you
so close the door on your way out
listen to me turn the lock from inside
a clicking that says
nothing
and everything

step away from the door while I
slide to the bottom
give me space while I cry
while I figure out why my heart is heavy
why my blood is boiling
why my skin is on fire
why I can't put feelings into thoughts into
words into phrases

so instead I will sit here at the bottom of
this door & let my heavy heart
keep me down keep me low keep me grounded

until my soul takes root and grows a floral
oasis. petals strong vibrant and wise
their wisdom thriving from the air around
you

the air that reminds you I locked the door and
didn't let you in

sun shiny blue skies
wrapped in warm air
get me out of my dark lonely basement

I like to wander across the street
to the local greenhouse
and peruse the flowers
analyzing the souls of each bud
to see which flower has the same
kind of wild yet sensitive spirit as me

I found myself standing
in front of vibrant green sprout
in a clay colored pot
the type of pots that remind girls
of gardening with their grandmothers

the tag on this prunella grandiflora read
self-healing perennial

when the air warms a bit more
I'll buy millions of prunella grandifloras
and spend the summer
surrounded by self healing flowers
so I can soak up their wisdom
and become whole again

I pray to get through this heartache

I yearn to sense fire and feel gratitude. to
know with certainty this flame is taking
everything. to know with reverence that
destruction of the present means space for
beauty in the future

I choose to live my life with this faith
flowing through my being. to see fire in my
life and know without a doubt

God is preparing a garden

a floral oasis for me to embrace my wildness
soak in God's beauty & feel the warmth of the
sun on my newly healed skin

flowers, fire & faith

there are so many endings in our story
I can't remember the beginning

except I'll never forget how we began

we were young and eager to be loved by
someone afraid of what that actually meant
our story is stained red with heartbroken
bleeding hearts and tinged grey with
disappointment

our story will reside in a sacred section of
my heart wrapped with wisdom I have gained
from our time apart and love I have learned to
have for myself

I will never again be made to stay small

I will go through this grief with all the
things I need to make it through and I will
come out wiser stronger braver armed with a
freedom I've never before had

I will never again settle for anything less
than whole love

take me to the water

sun glistened & sparkle
sing me a lullaby for my sorrows
rock my sadness to sleep

sing my soul a love song

pull me into your crystal blue & heal me
cover me with your deep soothe
promise me the pain will end

sing my soul a love song

show me how each future hope and dream
come to life
show me adventure
show me freedom

sing my soul a love song

take me to the water

watering flowers...

I am going to fill myself
with so much self-love
it will shine out my eyes
and provide me with protection
from those who are
incapable of treating me
with kindness empathy & compassion

with *lace* in her hair *flowers* in her heart &

freedom in her feet she promised herself to

always chase *fairy dust* fall in love with

sunsets & breathe with *bravery* in her ribs

Psalms 6:6

I am weary with my groaning all the night
make my bed to swim; I water my couch with my
tears
          (my couch, my bed, the shower, my car...)

Jeremiah 17:14

Heal me, O Lord, and I shall be healed; save me,
and I shall be saved: for thou art my praise
          (take this pain from me, I pray...)

Psalms 55:17

Evening, and morning, and at noon, will I
pray, and cry aloud, and he shall hear my
voice
          (God? It's me again...)

*verses are from the King James Version of
The Holy Bible*

I want to be standing in the crystal clear
water of authenticity & vulnerability
baring my soul and have a man be brave enough
to swim into the water with me

"*there you are*" I'll say
"*I've been waiting for you*"

he'll surround me with his gentle strength
and we'll swim to the depths of the pond
dissolving into each other's waves

I took a sledgehammer to mirrors
whose reflection told me I was less

than. I watched as their shattered
shards shimmered to the floor

picked up the pieces
created a dazzling disco ball

and danced myself whole

disco ball dance party

as I carefully stepped over it
a crack in a sidewalk
caught my attention

the damaged cinderblock
reminded me of myself

her bravely sprouted wildflowers
poking through her cracks
proving scars are a space for beauty

on the other side of this pain
there will be scars
where burns once were

I will take my newly formed heart
& treat it with the love I have
learned to have for myself

I don't regret
the promises I made on
that sunny fall day in the park

but having to pick
the last seams from our vows
has me wishing that
beautiful day in the park never happened

I want to be free

free of him. free of us

I want to be free of what I was before our
destruction placed me on a path of healing

I want to be free
but these seams are sewn
with a twisted diligence

picking them from my tapestry will require a
strength and perseverance I don't know I have

the eve before the sunrise

I don't realize how lonely I am
until the painfully strong desire
to snuggle in with the person beside me
(no matter who they are)
overwhelms me
attempting to weigh me down and
take my breath away

shoulders up, girl
take a deep breath
get yourself through the moment

I crave the nurturing touch of another

in my heart is a growing gratitude for a space
wherein I am allowed safety from his
negativity

a safety in which I thrive

a safety to breathe easy
go wherever I choose
embrace spontaneity
sit in reflective silence & surround myself
with love laughter & gratitude

a space to learn how to feel pain

a space to learn I am worthy of boundaries. of
the opportunity to think. to speak my peace
and be heard

a space to learn how to honor my intuition
and follow my heart. to love myself and stand
my ground

to learn the only person I need love from is me

a space to learn that I will be okay with
whatever happens in this forest

this space and its safety was a gift I was
given when he left and my gratitude for it
ever grows

when this forest ends,
there will just be another
to walk through

that is the nature of life

one forest & then
                another &
                        another &
                                another

each set of trees
            meadows
                    storms
                        wildflowers

        present to teach us what is needed to
        make it through the next forest

                                        wisdom

a meadow called

love...

not until my divorce did I learn that God paid
attention to me. that He cared for my safety.
that He loved me. I learned He would throw me
into the most challenging painful situations
in hopes I would learn what was needed for my
liberation

through and after and still I learn He works
tirelessly to save me from myself

...

a space around me arrived immediately after I
learned of his existence. I see now that this
space was an opening of my spirit. like she
knew her spirit partner was out there and she
was holding out for his arrival

I fought this space— ignored it. tried to
reject it. was terrified of it. but the space
always came back. try as hard as I did this
space was staying

my soul found her mate

I was always walking towards him. every
forest led me closer— I know that now. without
a doubt this man and I made plans before our
spirits came to this mortal life and everyone
and everything has been a stepping stone to
become who we needed to be for each other

he wraps his arms around me &
my black ice heart melts into a
vulnerable mess of hope & weak knees

my head becomes a haze filled cloud
his chest becomes the safest place
I've ever rested my weary spirit

desire joins fear in a battle
both to stay and to flee
I would run but my legs have turned into
noodles I would only collapse and pull him on
top of me we would escape into a world of
touch taste passion & breathe I have no power
here

I feel myself sink into him and I hear a sigh
come from me & I don't know what depths it has
come from but I am awake and I didn't know I
was sleeping but I know now and can I stay
here forever. my heart beats passion &
yearning & anticipation and I don't want to
leave him but this is as much bliss as I can
handle so I turn around & somehow

I walk into the house
put the flowers on the table
stumble to my room
intoxicated on his magic
lay on the floor and
marvel at the beauty of
not being able to stand

I have spent lifetimes in control
every move every step every word
carefully thought out calculated

every risk weighed

but now I want to throw caution to the wind
let go of it all
make a home out of his body
live there forever

how can a hug be so powerful

rooted in friendship
soul level understandings & eyes that are
home
honest conversations about our hearts
timing & faith
patience
compassion
commitment
mouths on mouths and hands on hearts

consistent
            the
                f
                 a
                  l
                   l
                    i
                     n
                      g

                                    together

he
can take
my breath away
&
bring me back
to life
with
the same kiss

what magic is his mouth made from

it wasn't so much falling off the wagon as it
was crouching down tying my shoes into the
tightest knot possible before leaping as far
away from The Man Wanting To Love Me

wanting to love me is precarious at best
wanting to love me is an odd mix of
frustration and determination
wanting to love me is resilience. deep
grounding breath. patience

wanting to love me is brave

because I spend a lot of time in a haze
walking around Walmart with last nights
hair. in sweatpants and a jean jacket drinking
too sweet to be good for me tea filling my
basket and head with everything but him

oooh yes. I do need those knives in my kitchen
...and that tea mug...and ...
...oh yep that popcorn popper

everything but him because he wants to love
me and I am terrified

I don't understand how a man would want to
love me
how a man would want to peel my layers and
lay with me in the dark. how a man would have
patience to wait for me to be ready

I don't understand how a man would want to
hold space for me while I dance my dance of

come undone-put self together-come undone
repeat

what does he see in me that I don't

damnit I'm crying in Walmart again
if I keep sipping my tea maybe no one will
notice

his voice does something to me. speaks to some
innermost part of my spirit lights me on fire
but the kind of fire that is soothing and
healing and grows the most beautiful flowers
like I've known him forever and my spirit has
been waiting for her partner and now he's here

he's here
and I'm crying in Walmart
scared to be loved
drinking too sweet to be good for me tea

I should probably buy new curtains

I wish I could enjoy the bliss he brings with
him but after his sentiments of love and
attraction have filtered through the junk in
my head the only message I hear is how I will
disappoint him

he will be disappointed
I am not enough
I am too much
he will see me and he will cringe
he won't stay because no one stays

I am disappointing
I am not enough
I am too much

he will be disappointed and he will leave me

one step forward, two steps back

even the steps backwards are steps forward

I have nothing to show for it
aside from dried flowers &
a heart full of yearning

was it real
or was I so desperate
I imagined the whole thing

if I peel back the books
will there be flowers as proof
or just paper with
a collection of words
lonelier than my heart

I hope we run into each other when the
sun is shining

I hope we'll be happy to see each other
excited even. a little nervous too

my eyes will remind you of love & magic
your eyes will remind me of passion & safety

I hope we go for coffee. americano & a tea latte
I hope the air smells sweet & hopeful like
our reunion
I hope love is present that day
I hope she brings her dear friend swooning
I hope you'll be okay
I hope when I look at you I'll know
our time is finally here

I hope my unknowing search for you in
everyone else will stop because I will have
found you at the right time instead

I hope you hold my hand in
my favorite bookstore
I hope our dreams turn into reality
I hope we put a piano in a van
I hope we find ourselves a backyard full of
wildness and adventure. trees & twinkly
lights. contentment & companionship.
grace & God.
I hope we do all the things we said we would
two daydreamers in a big messy world
looking for love looking for peace
looking for each other

you take the photos and I'll write the words

we'll make art and love and magic
we'll immerse ourselves in each other on a
blanket under the moon drinking tea writing
poems about the stars. we'll wake up early so
you can capture the perfect sunrise. we'll
frame it and know the rest of our lives
together will be captured in moments of color
and wisps of light
we'll have a secret book of photos and poems
and flowers

I hope when we're old and grey we'll reminisce
about that day we ran into each other. about
how you held my hand in our favorite
bookstore. how we went for coffee. and how we
knew our time had finally come

winter

he pulled me in &
taught me about a softness
I hadn't known about

how does he do that

touch me for the first time
but feel like home

spring

I will blissfully spend lifetimes with him
snuggled under feather printed blankets
taking afternoon naps on couches
our love as loud as the rolling thunder
outside the open window

summer

the sky a deep garden of stars and dreams

me and him under the same moon always

teary eyed goodbyes and hugs that last
eternities

elastic hearts stretched over miles of
highway

a flame split in two

fall

a dark room and him
our heartbeats connected to
the echo of the other
our souls weary from the world
refueling on touch & stillness & breath

during the night he reaches for my hand
& our energy sparks my palm
he takes my hand into his and I curl into him
our bodies entwine lighting my skin on fire

how can we possibly sleep with all this
lightning in our sheets?

in the morning he pours honey into my tea
with eyes that know details
and hands that know direction

my knees as weak as my tea is sweet

nightmare

the flowers burn
the beauty I once found freedom in
no longer exists
the meadow I loved is obliterated by
a raging flood of heartbreak

lightning strikes the tree
fills it with ash & isolation
walls appear from skeletons of love past
I prepare for battle

the tree dies
nothing grows again
grief overtakes me
I stop breathing
I die

my body rests in the burnt embers of flowers
that once grew from my scars

 eyes open. deep breath. hand on heart. beating

stormy day in the meadow

we're wrapped around each other
discussing our recent difficulty
these moments are always my favorite

he says:

you are a beautiful storm & I love that about
you. you are power & beauty & passion

his eyes twinkle

and I happily lose myself in the rumble of
your thunder but sometimes liz, your
lightning...

he puts his hand on his chest & looks up at the
ceiling

... being struck by your lightning hurts

I imagine God watching us from wherever He is
cheering us on while we work through these
things

this man communicates with me in a way my
soul understands. finding a companion whose
heartspeak is the same as mine is a blessing so
large I cannot fully comprehend how loved I
feel from God for being given this man as a
partner

one time while fighting I had one of those out
of body things happen where I temporarily saw
the whole scene and it was here I saw the
consequence of my brutality on this man I

love so sacredly

I need to learn how to be gentle. I need to
learn how to be gentle because I was bred in a
lion's den. I was raised to fight and to do so
viciously. I was taught to spare no one

but here is a man who communicates with the
same heartspeak as I do. here is a man who
loves freedom as much as I and whose natural
response to struggle just like me is to run
and despite all of that he is unwaveringly
committed to our relationship. to me

he ignores the wings on his shoes. the
unceasing urge to run. instead he wraps
himself around me and speaks from his heart.
he consistently grants me grace & compassion
& forgiveness

I need to shoot my lightning elsewhere

learn and grow

let's bring our wildness &
wear our sleeves with the hearts
our faith in God lighting the way
on an adventure in the forest

we'll lay in greenery
gaze up at the stars
fall asleep wrapped around each other
make love as the sun rises &
use her light to find the perfect meadow

we'll stand in reverent silence
joined by touch faith and love

the meadows heartbeat will
join the rhythm of ours &
we'll be one in floral fragrant beauty

One cool summer morning in late August, while the sun prepared for her winter rest, a boy and his girl went on a bittersweet walk through the woods. Hand in hand, they marveled at the beauty of nature, both connected to the roots of the trees, the freedom in the sky & the solitude of the stars. They listened to owls in the trees above them, felt the dance of the river in their souls, and spoke candidly about the state of their hearts.

Summer was kind to them, gifting them with more time together than they imagined possible, considering all those miles between them. The boy and his girl sat shoulder to shoulder on a park bench made just for that moment, looked out at the river and felt a mix of things— gratitude, connectedness, love, God, apprehension, and sadness.

They were about to step into the unknown— as they rested in this place, in the beginning of this wave of uncertainty, along with gratitude for one another and for God, in their hearts they gathered their deep resounding connection to each other with the faith they would survive this wave.

While the boy and his girl promised to do their best to honor their love, they collected leaves freshly let go from their tall friends, each one an example of how their love would not only survive this wave, but thrive, providing new opportunities for beauty and life.

Oh, how they loved the imperfections of the leaves, for they knew their own flaws were beautiful.

Four months later, on the last day of the year, having survived the wave, the boy and his girl blissfully sat together with their beloved leaves. He thanked her for everything she was & she returned to him the gratitude.

They knew they were about to go into another wave of uncertainty, so again the boy and his girl spoke candidly about the state of their hearts –how this journey into the unknown taught them, healed them, held them with grace & brought them closer.

how they were grateful.
how they were in love.
how– like the leaves they collected four short but long months ago– they were given new opportunities for beauty and growth.
how they would not only survive– but thrive– growing closer with every challenge.

As they enjoyed this short blissful moment together, the boy and his girl lovingly placed the leaves in a frame. Something to treasure when nights are lonely and the path is unclear.

Something to honor the connectedness they

feel within nature & to each other.
Something to represent the unique beauty
their love is.

The boy and his girl parted ways after
the last day of the year willingly stepping
into the next wave of uncertainty. They didn't
know where life would take them but they were
holding onto faith & the love in the leaves.

a cottonwood and his wildflower

have we forgotten.

touches like heaven on our tired lonely skin
voids of ache filled with tenderness
brave solitude nurtured with compassion &
understanding
solid brick walls built with diligent
stubbornness turned into heaps of sand with a
glance a touch a kiss
soul friends
passionate love made in sheets. in dark. in
light
a soundtrack of poems playing in the
background- the only way to describe how we
feel when the feeling is so big and the words
so small

we are everything good we have waited for
worked for. prayed for
we are nights on backroads under stars
sipping tea from a thermos.
we are daydreams of our future. our own earth.
less space between. home
we are adventures in trees guided by sunsets.
we are commitment companionship
accountability
we are a floral oasis. wild strong & ruthless
believers of freedom

we are everything

                    there is not enough

not enough time
not enough mornings
not enough together
not enough touch
not enough mouths
not enough play
not enough eyes

not enough soul soothing hugs
not enough

        will we forget

when distance between us stretches too long
when life keeps us too busy
when our voids refill with ache and our sand
hardens into brick

this poem wrote itself in segments. in prayers offered. sentiments expressed. wisdom absorbed. seeds lovingly left in the soil of my transformative journey

moon

the night of the superbloodwolfmoon I stood under her red brilliance and felt her powerful pull. she humbly hid behind the clouds that night, but I stood in the crisp winter air, in awe of her reverent power

the next morning as I stifled my sadness, a picture flew off the wall

dandelion

the wise old dandelion embraces the wind and bravely shares pieces of herself with the world, while fiercely remaining firm in the earth

I think my soul is a dandelion

shake off those leaves, bravegirl

for months my mantra was to be brave in love. and then in a quiet moment of prayer and meditation I realized that being brave in love had very little to do with whomever was in my future and everything to do with me. absorbing this wisdom changed the trajectory I was on.

I will always strive to stand tall, take
chances & love myself first. and when I falter,
because I will, I will grant myself the grace
needed to grow

soulmates

I don't know what I believe to be true about
soulmates. I just know that man is my spirit's
partner

humanity

I will love him through all the quirks
humanity offers so I can enjoy his spirit in
eternity

independence

equally important to knowing that
companionship is a possibility this universe
is offering me is the ability to stand strong
on my own

to nourish my roots. nurture my independence

wildness

wildness is soft. softness is wild. and on goes
the most liberating circle you will find
yourself in

about the author

Elizabeth Ann is a tea drinking, poem writing, enthusiast of the trees. She loves creating- from painting to sewing & writing to fiber arts- and the feel of the earth between her toes.

Elizabeth also loves people- when she's not with her children or writing, she's working for an organization supporting adults with disabilities. Elizabeth is looking forward to a time when her love of serving people and her passion for writing merge with one another.

She dreams of a life with a little less hustle and a little more adventure, but until then you can find her writing in dark corners at the end of her always busy days and daydreaming about cruising around in classic Wagoneers & living in VW buses with her man in the middle of forests with twinkle lights wrapped around trees.

You can also find Elizabeth on social media:

twitter: @lizzydanger
Instagram: @lizzydanger
Poetizer: @ Elizabeth Ann
Wordpress: www.lizzydanger.wordpress.com

thank you

Made in the USA
Middletown, DE
20 March 2019